# PULLMAN PRIDE

## Photographs from the archive of E J Morris - Company Secretary of the Pullman Car Company

In Loving Memory of Ted Morris

1904 - 1994

*N.B.*

# PULLMAN PRIDE

## Photographs from the archive of E J Morris - Company Secretary of the Pullman Car Company

## Compiled by John Morris and Antony Ford

ISBN  (10)  0 –9554110-1-7
(13) 978-0-9554110-1-4


First published in 2007 by Kevin Robertson
under the **NOODLE BOOKS** imprint
PO Box 279
SOUTHAMPTON
SO32 3ZX

www.kevinrobertsonbooks.co.uk

Printed in England by
The Amadeus Press
Cleckheaton
West Yorkshire

*Front cover - top: Rebuilt 'Battle of Britain' class No 34088 '213 Squadron' ready at London Victoria with the down 'Golden Arrow' service on 22 July 1960. (Tony Molyneaux)*

*Front cover - lower: Car No 34 forming part of the 'Bournemouth Belle' set on the last day of service, 9th July 1967, at Southampton Central. (Collection Bob Winkworth)*

*Rear cover: The Queen, Duke of Edinburgh, Princess Margaret and Anthony Armstrong-Jones, Prime Minister Harold Wilson and other dignitaries welcome Queen Juliana of the Netherlands from the Royal Train, including a Golden Arrow Kitchen Car, possibly 'Orion', at Victoria Station. The locomotive is electric No 20003.*

*Preceding pages: The 'Thanet Belle' shown passing Swanley in 1948. This all-Pullman train consisted mostly of - class Cars converted from ambulance coaches in 1920-21 after service in the First World War. The unrebuilt Bulleid locomotive looks as though it is burning its share of 'nutty slack' coal as it speeds its train between Victoria and Margate via Faversham, Canterbury and Deal.*

# Contents

*"The 'Southern Belle' Pullman Limited Train. 'The Last Word in Luxury Travel'. Victoria and Brighton in 60 Minutes - Weekdays and Sundays." (Contemporary Postcard and Caption)*

# Introduction

After his retirement from The Pullman Car Company in 1967, John's father, Ted Morris, was invited to talk to various organisations, ranging from the Retired Railway Officers' Society to the Railway Club at Kingsbury School, Dunstable, where John was then Head of the Geography Department.

The text of the 'Pullman Story' on the following pages is based closely on the typed notes for those talks. However, any elaboration deemed necessary has been included for the purposes of accuracy. Ted left the notes carefully filed in a scrapbook together with a personal but quite large collection of documents, photographs and other Pullman memorabilia. John has selected the best of these and prepared the captions and commentary, with the very able assistance of Antony Ford, secretary and curator of The Pullman Society. We hope that the illustrations speak volumes in themselves.

Of course, the views expressed in this book are solely those of the authors. We hope that we have managed to capture something of a bygone age of railway travel which has gone forever. The album is necessarily selective and by no means comprehensive; interested readers are directed to other books that are available for detailed historical information. Some of these are listed in the Further Reading section of this volume. New evidence is constantly coming to light even though most of the original records stored at the Victoria Station offices were destroyed in the Blitz.

Ted's children, Jill and John, remember with affection and gratitude, their childhood journeys in comfort by Pullman. This may have been a rare trip on the "Arrow", as a prelude to a holiday in France, Corsica or Switzerland. It may have been just one of those day visits to the south coast of England for bracing walks along the promenade of one seaside resort or the other. The family would have been rewarded later with tea and 'lashings of hot toast, simply oozing with butter', in the coupé on the way home. However, for Ted's wife, Elsie, 'Pullman' meant late evenings for him at the Office or his being shut away for hours on end in the dining room as he wrestled with column after column of neatly written figures.

We hope you will enjoy sharing with us a journey down memory lane as you turn the pages that follow.

John Morris and Antony Ford

Note - Unless otherwise stated all photographs are from the collection of E J Morris.

# Glossary

**Antimacassar** - Covering put on the backs of chairs as protection from grease or as an ornament.
**Belle** - A handsome woman. First used by Pullman in 1908.
**Car** - Railway carriage. (American parlance.)
**Composite** - Describing a Car with accommodation for classes, first and third (second) and occasionally third.
**Coupé** - An enclosed part of a first-class Car designed to seat a minimum of four and a maximum of six in some privacy.
**Cuspidor** - Spittoon.
**Damask silk** - Kinds of figured, woven material of silk or linen especially white table linen with designs shown by incidences of light.
**Hassock** - Footstool.
**Marquetry** - Decorative inlaid work in wood veneers.
**Moquette** - Material of wool on cotton, with pile or loops, used for upholstery. ("Cut" or "Uncut".)
**Ormolu** - Gold-coloured alloy of copper, zinc and tin. (French influence.)
**Supplement** - Fee additional to the fare payable for travelling in a Pullman Car.
**Vestibule** - The enclosed entrance to a railway-carriage.

*Ted was a member of the Transportation Club. In September 1958, the Club Committee, of which he was a member, were photographed with the then Minister of Transport, Harold Watkinson. Back Row: Col Mulligan (Sec), Mr Goodhead, Mr Castle, Mr Cooke, Mr Wilmot, Mr Webb, Mr James and Mr Hearn; Front Row: Ted Morris, Mr Royle, Harold Watkinson (Minister of Transport), Mr Handover, Mr Grand, General Szlumper.*

# Ted's Pullman Life

Born: 27th December, 1904.

Pupil at Mitcham Lane L.C.C. School, 1912 – 1918.

Started as a messenger boy with the Pullman Car Company Ltd: 1st February, 1921.

Studied at Regent Street Polytechnic: Company Secretarial and Accountancy Course.

Appointed Accountant to the Company: 1927/28.

Formed and operated, as part of his duties as Accountant, a subsidiary company (Irish Pullmans Limited) to operate Pullman Cars on the Great Southern Railway in Ireland for eight years ending 1935. The Company ran services from Dublin to Limerick, Cork and Sligo. He acted as liquidator of this subsidiary Company in 1937.

Appointed Assistant Company Secretary and Chief Accountant in 1936.

Company Secretary and Chief Accountant in 1940.

General Manager in 1962.

*Right: Pullman Car Secretary, Ted Morris, at his Victoria Station office during the 1930s with not even an adding machine in sight.*

*George Mortimer Pullman (centre) posing with members of his family. (The original photograph seems to have been slightly re-touched; all eyes have rather prominent pupils - perhaps they had become blurred due to movement while the subjects endured a lengthy time exposure.)*

## 1859

**"OLD No. 9" THE FIRST PULLMAN CAR** The first Pullman sleeper, built 1859, was a reconstructed day coach, 40 feet long or about half the present length. Except wheels and axles, it was practically all wood. The roof was flat and so low a tall man was liable to bump his head. The seats were immovable; two small wood-burning stoves furnished heat. Lighted with candles, it had at each end a small toilet room large enough for one person, with tin wash basin in the open and water from the drinking faucet. There were ten upper and ten lower berths; mattresses and blankets, but no sheets. But it was the best yet.

# THE PULLMAN STORY

The Pullman story started way back in 1858, when, after a particularly cold and uncomfortable journey, the idea of lessening the hardships of railway travel occurred to one George Mortimer Pullman. At that time he ran a cabinet and joinery business in Albion, New York.

Pullman persuaded the Chicago and Alton Railroad to allow him to reconstruct the interiors of two 49-foot (Pullman Progress says "40-foot long") cars to provide upholstered sleeping berths. Following the completion of these experiments in reconstruction and their quick acceptance by the travelling public, Pullman was encouraged to build new cars incorporating his own ideas with upper and lower berths and many embellishments to both interiors and exteriors. The operation of these early vehicles soon brought success, and with it the demand by other railroads to contract with Pullman to supply and operate Sleeping Cars to his design.

The standardisation of rail track gauges in 1867 by the several railroad companies operating in America at that time stimulated the growth of the company formed by Pullman under the rather grandiose name of Pullman's Palace Car Company, to be later re-named The Pullman Company. A number of workshops were built on the land of these railroad companies but were later consolidated on some 4000 acres purchased by Pullman in the suburbs of Chicago. On this land, Pullman developed his own brand of social reform, building not only workshops but houses for his work staff, a school, a church and other amenities. He called it Pullman City. The scheme attracted much criticism and its administration was eventually taken over and absorbed into the City of Chicago. One can imagine some hard bargaining on both sides.

The first Restaurant Car was introduced to operate in conjunction with the Pullman sleepers, followed by the first parlour cars with what were at the time, the quite revolutionary swivel type seats of the small armchair sort. Drinks and refreshments were served at the seats.

At this time two other entrepreneurs, Mann and Wagner, tried their hand at railway carriage building. Both formed companies to build and operate sleeping cars. Wagner was soon out of the race, while Mann found that he could not get very far in this activity without infringing the various patents that had been developed the hard way by Pullman. Long and costly lawsuits followed which finally helped Pullman to take over operations across America and into Canada. In point of fact, Mann meantime managed to get into Europe before Pullman, signing a contract with the Belgian Wagons-Lits Company. In quite a short time this contract was taken over by Pullman. The door to Europe was now open to Pullman's fertile brain and a contact already made in Britain was possibly exploited. James (later to become Sir James) Allport, the General Manager of The Midland Railway paid a visit to the United States and was very interested in the development of rolling stock in America. This interest was fostered by a personal appearance by Pullman himself at the Annual General Meeting of the Midland Railway Company. Allport convinced the Directors and so, in 1873, Pullman's cars were introduced into Britain.

The Midland decided to take on to their lines some 13 Sleeping Cars, 20 Parlour Cars and one Dining Car named "Prince of Wales" - thirty-four vehicles in all. It is interesting to note that 37 cars were built by Pullman in America and shipped to England for assembly in the Derby Works. They comprised 16 Sleeping Cars, 20 Parlour Cars and one Dining Car. A document in Ted's possession shows them to have been the property of The Car Syndicate Limited in the first instance, an English company with some obvious connection with America by shareholding. Ted had no records of the business transacted in these early operations but in 1881 "Pullman's Palace Car Company" took over these thirty-four Cars together with four others

*Pullman Pride - the epitome of service and which continued the standards of the Edwardian era unchanged in an ever changing world.*
*This particular illustration is from a contemporary LBSCR colour booklet and shows a smartly dressed Pullman attendant who would have brought a previously-ordered meal to your seat.*

*A grand lady, no doubt well able to afford the supplementary fare, boards a Pullman Car, her bag carried by a junior porter. A conductor, identified by his long, double-breasted coat supervises.*

allocated to the Alta Italian Railway Company. That same year the latter four Cars, three of them Sleeping Cars, were in fact employed in the Meridionale Railway Company operating, Ted believed, between Bologna and Brindisi. Thus Pullman's Palace Car Company had well and truly arrived in Europe. The copy of the employment agreement (Page 21), is a small reminder of the everyday work required to run the Company.

On the Midland Railway, Pullmans operated smoothly from 1881 until 1888 when the Midland decided not to renew the Pullman Contract. A considerable amount of hard bargaining ensued. George Pullman's offer to sell 14 Cars for £30,000 was summarily reduced to the first quoted figure by the Midland of £20,000, which he was, as Ted saw, forced to accept. This type of transaction was repeated in 1933 when the London, Midland and Scottish Railway decided to cancel the Pullman Contract for operating north of the Border that had been made years earlier with the Caledonian. It was not practicable to transfer the Cars, which were 63 feet 10 inches by 9 feet to use on the more restricted gauge of the London and North Eastern and Southern Railways' steam-hauled services. After some very bitter correspondence and negotiations, in which Ted was personally involved, 20 Pullman Cars allocated to the Caledonian Railway were eventually purchased by the Midland for £21,000.

Until Pullman's four-wheeled bogies were introduced into Britain, the sight of a railway carriage on eight wheels was unprecedented. No-one at that time thought of doubting the stability of a carriage with only four points of support, for, with true conservatism, nobody has seen the need to better the 'construction' of a horse which after all does very well with one leg at each corner. The first fifteen-year contract made by Pullman with the Midland was similar in many respects to later ones with other railway companies. In these contracts, the railways had the free use of the various types of Cars introduced while at the same time maintaining the running gear. The Pullman Company in its turn retained the revenue derived from the sale of sleeping berths, seating and refreshments.

The Derby workshops were used at this time to construct and alter the layout of Pullman Cars. During the period of this first Contract, 1881 to 1888, only a non-contractual agreement existed, whereby two Pullman Sleeping Cars operated out of Kings Cross together with a Parlour Dining Car called the "Prince of Wales". Incidentally, Ted believed this to have been an irritant to the Midland Company and a partial cause of the breakdown in the relationship between Pullman and the Midland. Later there was to be a separate contract with the Caledonian Railway Company (afterwards absorbed into the London, Midland and Scottish Railway).

In 1885, a Contract with the Highland Railway was concluded. Two Cars "Balmoral" and "Dunrobin" were built at Derby and allocated to the Inverness - Glasgow route. They continued to run regularly there until 1906 when it seems the Highland had prepared the way for cancellation of the Contract by building their own sleepers. They also intimated that they were not anxious to buy the two Pullmans. The Cars were of curious construction being only 36 feet 3 inches long and weighing 16 and a half tons with access to the coaches by a centre door opening outwards, no doubt built to specific requirements. Hamilton Ellis wrote in the "Railway Magazine" that these Cars had been built into a bungalow at Seaford where they still existed in 1958 within the shell of the building. This way of making use of Cars withdrawn from traffic became universal in Britain until the advent of stricter town and country planning legislation. (One complete car exists today and parts of the other.)

In 1882 an English company called the Pullman Company Ltd. was formed but under American control. In 1905 (Muhl and Klein say 1908), the control of the Company passed into English hands as a public company under the chairmanship of financier and banker, Davison Dalziel (afterwards to become Sir Davison Dalziel and later Lord Dalziel of Wooler). In September, 1915 he founded a new Pullman Car

# THE PULLMAN STORY

Company Ltd in London under his own directorship. The Compagnie Internationale des Wagons Lits had a significant holding in this Company by 1925 at the latest.

The London Brighton and South Coast Railway was the first to link up with Pullman in the South. The Contract signed in 1877 between the Palace Car Company and the Brighton Company was continued with the American-controlled English Pullman Company Ltd through its successor, the wholly English-owned Drawing Room Cars Company Ltd. This became finally the Pullman Car Company and remained so until 1932, when the original Contract formed the basis of a new one with the Southern Railway embodying in it the new all-electric Pullman Cars, including of course, the three "Brighton Belle" Units. These Units were the successors to the loco-hauled "Southern Belle". A fleet of Cars, including the magnificent "Grosvenor" and "Bessborough", had been constructed specially for the Southern Belle. The motive power in the Belle units was the property of the Railway; Pullman, as such, never owned at any time any form of railway locomotion.

It was on the Brighton Railway that electric lighting on Pullman trains brought another "first" for railways in Britain.

In 1882, the London, Chatham and Dover Railway Company agreed, as an experiment in introducing luxury travel to their lines, to operate Pullman's Parlour Car "Jupiter", transferred from the London, Brighton and South Coast Railway. It was transferred back in July 1884. According to a copy of the Contract in Ted's possession, Pullmans did not run on the South Eastern Railway until 1909 and then only between London and Dover. In 1912, they extended their services to include Folkestone Pier from Charing Cross as well as Dover from both Charing Cross and Victoria. Services were also introduced to major South Coast resorts.

The London and South Western Railway contracted in 1889 to run a limited number of single Pullman Parlour Cars on the Waterloo to Bournemouth route for a period of some 20 years. It appears they were not an outstanding success; it is a fact of life that Pullman, of itself, does not easily compete with ordinary passenger stock. This factor became most evident with the withdrawal of the loco-hauled Pullmans on the Brighton lines which before electrification were only gangwayed to each other where one or more Cars were formed in the train; passenger access was thus denied from the rest. The all-Pullman "Bournemouth Belle" proved the point. Introduced in 1931, it became a popular success. Also at this time, Pullman Boat Trains were put into traffic on the Southampton Docks service to link with the transatlantic liner services starting there. They scored an early success especially with American passengers and continued to do so until air traffic across the Atlantic reduced passenger loadings into Southampton to the point where they became uneconomic as first-class traffic.

The year 1909 saw the introduction of two Pullman Cars on the Metropolitan Railway operating some eight services every weekday to Rickmansworth, Chesham and Aylesbury from Baker Street. The Cars were standard, non-gangwayed, elliptical-roofed ones and they proved very popular with the City businessman and the theatregoer. Mr Gulbenkian, the millionaire, was a regular traveller. The Contract had no stated life but in fact terminated at the beginning of the Second World War in 1939. The Cars were requisitioned by the Timber Control people, used as accommodation offices, and ended their days as bungalows.

A Contract with the Caledonian Railway was signed in 1914, an unfortunate time as, within months, the first ten Cars designed for the service were withdrawn for the period of the First World War. In 1919 the working was resumed and additional Cars were gradually brought into traffic. Pullman Cars and Pullman Restaurant Cars were operated as a complete section under the supervision of a superintendent. The year 1933 saw the termination of the Contract and no Pullmans operated on the Midland until 1960 when the Blue Diesel Pullman commenced to run between Manchester and St. Pancras.

*A smartly turned-out conductor waits besides his car.*
*This and the preceding two views are reproduced from "Pullman and Perfection on the London, Brighton and South Coast Railway". Before the world reeled from the effects of the Great War, 1914-18, the booklet, probably dating from 1908, gives us some idea of the opulent nature of travel that reflected an optimistic time at the beginning of the century.*

# PULLMAN PRIDE

The Contract with the Great Eastern Railway was made in 1919 and first and third class Pullman Cars, either singly or in pairs, operated from Liverpool Street Station to Cambridge, Clacton and other places on the East Coast. The "Hook Continental" also had first and second class Pullmans in its formation with marked success. With the Grouping and the emergence of the London and North Eastern Railway, the original Great Eastern Contract formed the basis of the introduction, or perhaps it should be said, the re-introduction of Pullman services on to northern routes to Scotland and the industrial cities.

Starting with the "Harrogate Pullman" to Leeds and Harrogate, Pullman services were later extended to Newcastle and eventually Edinburgh and Glasgow as the "Queen of Scots". From 1923 onwards, the Great Eastern section introduced a Sunday Clacton service. This later became the very popular "Eastern Belle" which ran to a different East Coast town each day.

Pullman owes its successful integration into railway operation to its ability to adapt itself to public requirements as interpreted by railway managements. Ted Morris instances two such examples: the conversion of the first class Pullmans on the Margate and Ramsgate services to composite first and third class accommodation, and the building of six specially constructed Cars in 1926 to run on the Charing Cross, Tunbridge Wells and Hastings line which had a very narrow loading gauge. At the

*Combined American-built Pullman Sleeping and Saloon Car of the late Nineteenth Century. Note the elaborately decorated undersides of the upper berths in their day-time positions. The original oil lamps had, by this time, replaced the candles used in earlier cars. (Deutsches Museum, München.)*

# THE PULLMAN STORY

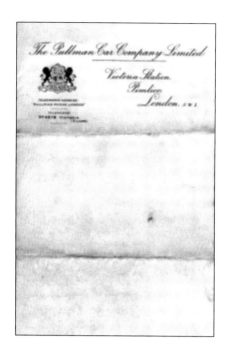

start these Cars were first class only but again, to meet demand, were converted to first and third class Composite Cars.

Between the Wars, Special Party traffic trains were developed and again Pullman produced converted Cars called Supply Cars to enable large numbers to be served their refreshments on their trips to the South Coast.

In 1926 four third class Pullman Cars were contracted to the Great Southern Railway in Ireland to operate between Dublin, Cork, Sligo and Limerick. (Ted Morris formed and operated a subsidiary company as part of his duties as Accountant to the Pullman Car Company.) This Company was called Irish Pullmans Ltd and had its offices and stores at Kingsbridge (now Dublin Heuston) Station. The four Cars were standard loading gauge but were re-bogied to enable them to run on the 5 feet 3 inch track. The Contract with the GSR was terminated at the end of ten years and the Cars sold to the Railway Company which ran them for a period as Supplementary Fare Cars and subsequently as Restaurant Cars.

At the end of the First World War, the Company continued its building programme but at high capital cost, making life difficult in the "slump" years. Share capital reconstruction followed to enable the Company to have a fairly smooth run up to the Second World War.

That was a real testing time for all concerned. All Pullman services were withdrawn for a short period, but, with an ingenious fitting to black out the windows, the electric Pullmans were back in their units for a couple of years. However, with the intensity of the bombing including a direct hit on the Brighton Belle units and much other damage, only some loco-hauled Cars remained in service. These operated from The Airways platform at Victoria in specially-formed trains of three Pullman Cars and a brake van, and ran at short notice to either Poole or Bournemouth for the flying boats ferrying V.I.P.s and training aircrews to and from Canada, and later, the United States. It earned the name "Ghost Train" as it invariably departed from the far end of Platform 17 at Victoria, with the passengers being discreetly ushered through the special B.O.A.C. (British Overseas Airways Corporation) doors leading into their terminal station.

On a number of occasions, due to delay at the coast stations, a second formation was called for. Ted Morris then acted as conductor with a scratch crew consisting of the Pullman Stores Manager and two of his assistants, who had been retained during the War, together with the spare chef, who was probably resting after a previous over-night run. On more than one occasion, no chef was available; the order of the day then was a "cold" menu. With America becoming involved in the War, this so-called "Ghost Service" gradually ceased.

Churchill had a modified coupé in Pullman Car "Ione", with special lock and blinds to ensure complete privacy and security, for use on inspection trips to various centres in the South. (Ted Morris commented many years later: "I may say that I do not think that he was aware of rationing for he always demanded his piece of cheese. In spite of my pleas at the Food Office, I was quite unable to obtain any special grant. On a couple of occasions, my own two ounces came up from home to the rescue.") The American Army Transportation Corps asked Ted Morris to provide a Pullman for the use of their chief officers. The arrangement was concluded one morning at 7.30 a.m. in their office in the Selfridge building. Car "Joan" (pronounced "Jo Ann" by our American cousins) was fitted up complete with office and plug-in telephone. The car was marshalled into many trains, together with a North Eastern sleeper, and ran to many ports and military centres from the Highlands of Scotland to the West Country and Dover. General Eisenhower travelled in this Car on a number of occasions with the American transport personalities, Colonels Ross and Ryan. Pullman car staff were often away from home for a week at a time. The provision of victuals came from many a strange source of supply.

5

# THE PULLMAN STORY

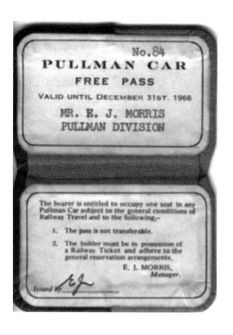

At the end of the Second World War, the Company found itself with over 100 cars damaged by enemy action. However, by restoring its own workshops to full production, and with the considerable help and co-operation of railway workshops, many of the pre-war Pullman and buffet car services were restored on the Southern and North Eastern by early 1946. Much of the Pullman records were destroyed in the last war - Hitler had three attempts to do this and nearly succeeded. Ted had some old documents in a file in his office at Victoria Station that he was able to recover although many had the marks of being baked in their steel cabinet.

Twenty-nine all-steel cars were refurbished and put into traffic on the "Queen of Scots", "Yorkshire Pullman", and latterly the "Tees-Tyne Pullman". The Post-war era saw the introduction of Buffet Cars which were operated at the request of the Southern on its Central and Eastern sections in place of Pullman Car services.

The opportunity for developing a holiday service to Devon was quickly seized. Thus came about the "Devon Belle" which was formed of two all-Pullman trains including two Observation Cars that had been converted from two third class Pullmans at the Company's Workshops. A Bar Car was created in a similar way for use in the "Golden Arrow" Pullman Train.

This was the time when visiting royalty and other dignitaries to the United Kingdom still travelled by ship or boat and then by train to London. The special Pullman train was the obvious choice for the final stage of the journey with Victoria being the arrival point.

In 1954, the Ordinary Share Capital was purchased by British Railways and there then followed, in 1955, the introduction of the "South Wales Pullman" serving Cardiff and Swansea. This was a success from the outset, paving the way for the Blue Pullman Diesel trains which followed in 1960. The "South Wales Pullman" was a new breakthrough from the experiment with the Great Western Ocean Liner Pullman and the Torquay and Plymouth all-Pullman service which had lasted a year in 1929. A tragedy in a way but for some reason, the Company's officials never developed a good rapport with their opposite numbers on the Great Western.

*1964-1966 leather bound Pass issued to Ted Morris by himself! Such was the power of the Company Secretary and Accountant!*

In 1959, five diesel-electric multiple unit Pullman trains were built, at the Company's cost, in the works of the Metro-Cammell Company. The units went into service on the Midland Region from London to Manchester and, with a mid-day service, to Nottingham. On the Western Region, other units took over the "South Wales Pullman" - from 1961, and services to Bristol and Birmingham. All proved highly successful although, as is the case with all unit trains, whenever even a slight breakdown occurred in one of the vehicles, the whole unit would have withdrawn. The original "South Wales" loco-hauled formation had been retained on the Western Region and so came in useful as a marvellous stand-by train from time to time.

With the eventual purchase of the Preference Shares by British Railways, the Company's activities were finally integrated into B.R., becoming a division of Hotels and Catering Services. As much as possible of the Pullman individuality was retained while at the same time activities were widened into restaurant car operation in selected timings. This continued until 1967 when it was decided to split up the Division with each Region to take over the Pullman services, and the Company ceased to operate as such.

Circa 1970 Ted wrote: "Mr Harding, the Managing Director, was retired from the Board and, for a few months, I held the post of General Manager as well as that of Director and Secretary of the Company. The object of the Hotel and Catering Division was to integrate the Pullman services into British Railways and to take into its orbit the Businessman's or Executive Restaurant Car operation."

Ted Morris ended one of his talks thus: "Looking back, I believe much was achieved in the development of rail travel by innovations in seating, lighting, décor and service. With its small, personally involved management, the Company was

*Opposite page: Woodcut of 1880 showing the interior of an English Pullman car. The American origins of the car are clearly seen: clerestory roof and small, low windows. (Deutsches Museum, München.)*

7

# PULLMAN PRIDE

*A 'Devon Belle' luggage label showing destinations of the Train, several of which are, of course, no longer accessible by any rail service. The artist was Kay Stewart.*

always able to adapt to change and fully co-operate with railway managements ensuring the minimum of delay in the implementation of new ideas. There were mistakes undoubtedly, for example, the introduction of two classes of Pullman. Although the second class car brought in a large part of the Company's revenue, the service given was by the same staff, the same menu and the same special running times; it was really illogical. I believe the Railway Companies and Regions should have given and extended the Pullman trains as a class of travel with prime timing with all the trimmings to justify a special fare. After all is said and done even today in the great levelling down of everything, we still have first class sections in aircraft, we have plush hotels and many other examples to prove there exists a demand for just that little extra."

"That Pullman had an impact on rail travel is undeniable. Whilst it cannot claim to be the inventor of the bogie, it certainly developed its design and from memory I recall the very smooth running of the six-wheeled bogies used on many Pullman Cars, Sleepers and Diners. The Pullman Gangway and Vestibule was introduced and was soon a universal fitting on all Pullman Car trains, although there still existed many Pullman Cars which were completely self-contained and were continued mainly to provide privacy from the rest of the train. With the adoption of the fitted covered gangway to ordinary rolling stock, where Pullmans were formed in the trains, some part of the "snob" value of Pullman, trading-wise, disappeared."

"Pullman had another attribute which lived on even after complete integration into British Railways, that of loyalty of purpose. Pullman is synonymous with personal service and pride of belonging to a personal organisation. I know this for a fact and practised it with success when given the task of integrating Pullman ideas into the Restaurant Car Service on the Executive Businessman's Services to which I have already referred. Restaurant Car employees, excellent men with many years experience on the Northern lines, I know at first resented Pullman intrusion. But I can say, without denial, that the Pullman uniform with its badges became a symbol to them of really belonging and identifying them with an outward sign of good service."

"Service brings reward both monetary and satisfaction. I believe that British Rail would recover much of its old image if more were made of the sense of pride in the job by a smart uniform and a more personal approach by management to be seen and not read about in so much paper exhortations. I remember vividly a trip I made circa 1970 in company with an Eastern manager who had transferred to the Western - he was known and recognised by staff all along the line, both station and track."

# THE PULLMAN STORY

**Further Reading**

There are some excellent references to Pullman Cars, the Company, its services and the work force behind the scenes in some of the following books. Since some were written, much new, and, previously thought lost, material has come to light which has displaced some earlier notions expressed in older texts.

*Leaflet reminding 'Golden Arrow' passengers of the presence of 'The Trianon Cocktail Bar' as part of the service offered by the Train.*

| | | | |
|---|---|---|---|
| George Behrend | "Pullman in Europe" | Ian Allan | 1962 |
| F. Burtt and Beckerlegg | "Pullman and Perfection" | Ian Allan | 1948 |
| Don Carter, Joe Kent and Geoff Hart, Ed by Nick Wellings | "Pullman Craftsmen" | Queenspark Books | 1992 |
| Charles Fryer | "British Pullman Trains" | Silver Link Publishing | 1992 |
| A Hasenson | "The Golden Arrow" | Howard Baker | 1970 |
| R W Kidner | "Pullman Cars on the Southern 1875 -1972" (Later revised and updated under the title "Pullman Trains in Britain") | The Oakwood Press | 1987 Revised and updated edition 1998 |
| J P Lepage | "Les voitures Pullman 4001 / 4030 de la Compagnie Internationale des Wagons Lits" | | 1985 |
| Julian Morel | "Pullman" | David and Charles | 1983 |
| Pullman Car Company publication | "The Golden Way" | Arden Press / W H Smith | From around 1919 to 1942 |
| Renzo Perret | "Le Carrozze Pullman" | Ediziani Elledi | 1982 |
| Kevin Robertson | "Blue Pullman" | Kestrel Railway Books | 2005 |
| Shirley Sherwood | "Pullmans of the Venice Simplon Orient Express" | Illustrated London News Group | 1992 |

# THE ALBUM

## The Co-Authors

Antony Ford has been a life-long Pullman Car enthusiast and has been collecting memorabilia including table lamps, marquetry panels, tickets, fixtures and fittings, etc for over twenty-five years. He has travelled on many British and continental Pullman services including, as a child, the "'Bournemouth Belle', 'Brighton Belle' and into the 1970s, 'The South Wales Pullman', 'Hull Pullman', 'Liverpool Pullman', and 'Manchester Pullman' services. Antony is currently General Secretary and Curator of The Pullman Society and lives in Wiltshire.

John Morris is now retired but finds himself more active than ever. He spends some of his time as a volunteer porter at Ropley on the Watercress Line in Hampshire and lives not far away in Surrey.

*Group of London Brighton and South Coast railway officials at Brighton Station after the inaugural run of a regular all-Pullman train from London in December 1888. There had been Pullman Cars on Brighton trains since 1875 and an all-Pullman train was run in 1881 but discontinued the next year.*

*Twelve-wheeler Pullman Car, 'The Arundel', showing clear features of its American origin - clerestory roof, large 'drop' windows and the typical Pullman oval windows of the lavatory compartments.*

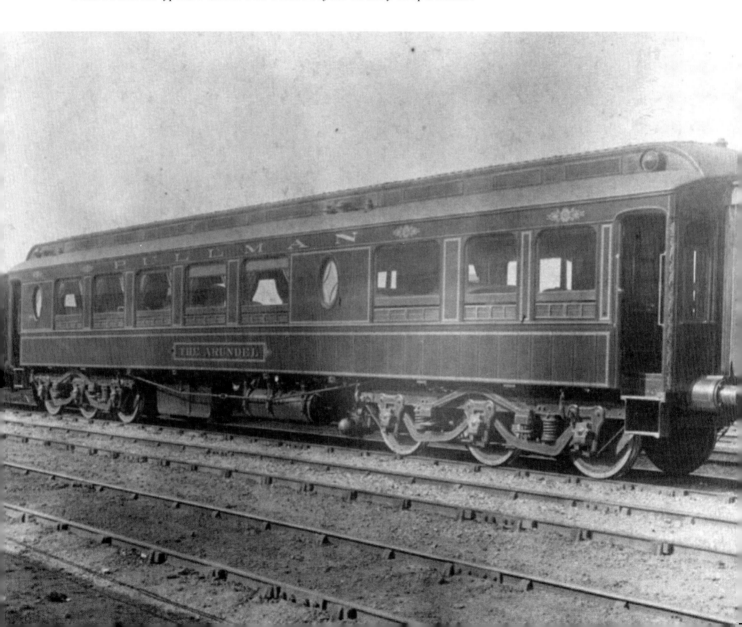

*Employment agreement between Pullman's Palace Car Company at St Pancras and Frederick Rous, dated 17 March 1882. Rous was to earn the princely wage of just 3/- per day as a Porter although this could no doubt be supplemented with tips. The grade was later changed to that of 'Attendant'.*

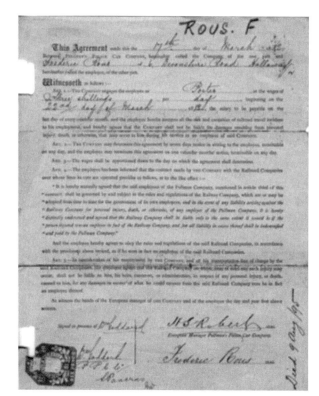

*An interior view of the First Class Pullman Car 'Grosvenor', built in 1908 for the 'Southern Belle' and showing the bar area and the leather upholstery of the generously–proportioned arm chairs. The Car survived in service until 1960 although towards the end it only saw occasional use in boat trains. The glass-fronted cabinet behind the bar displays various items for sale particularly cigars and confectionery. It was lockable, because there had been instances of silverware being stolen and everything had to be accounted for. (When the well-to-do could not be trusted not to slip a silver mustard pot into a pocket!) Note the cuspidors.*

This is but a brief description of the beauty which really makes this train unique in both elegance and luxury. Whatever brains were responsible for its design they did not overlook any tiny and seemingly insignificant detail. The very match-boxes fit into the scheme of things, and there is nothing to jar upon the most critical eye or the most fastidious taste.

The first revelation is enticing. The actual experience of the journey fulfils one's sense of satisfaction and pleasure. It has been said that the first choice of seats was difficult because of rival beauties, but that difficulty only lasts for the first few minutes, and invariably the passengers settle down, each one suiting his or her own taste, and particular desires.

These things depend upon circumstances. Two people for instance may wish for a tête-à- tête from London to Brighton. Certainly in this train a good providence befriends them. There are many cosy corners where two young people may sit at ease, in a snug way, and say to each other those vastly important things which belong to the philosophy of youth and love. On many of these journeys on "The Southern Belle" it is pleasant to see some of these young people, the girl pretty, and charmingly dressed, and with very bright eyes, the man, smart and well-groomed, seated together in one of the sheltered nooks on this fast express. As the train speeds on its way the sun shines through the window upon them, bathing them in its golden glamour. And if, as sometimes happens, they would rather be silent than talk, their eyes gaze out upon the fields that seem to fly by, upon lovely parklands and woodlands, and then upon the rolling downs that come before the journey's end.

(Continued page 22)

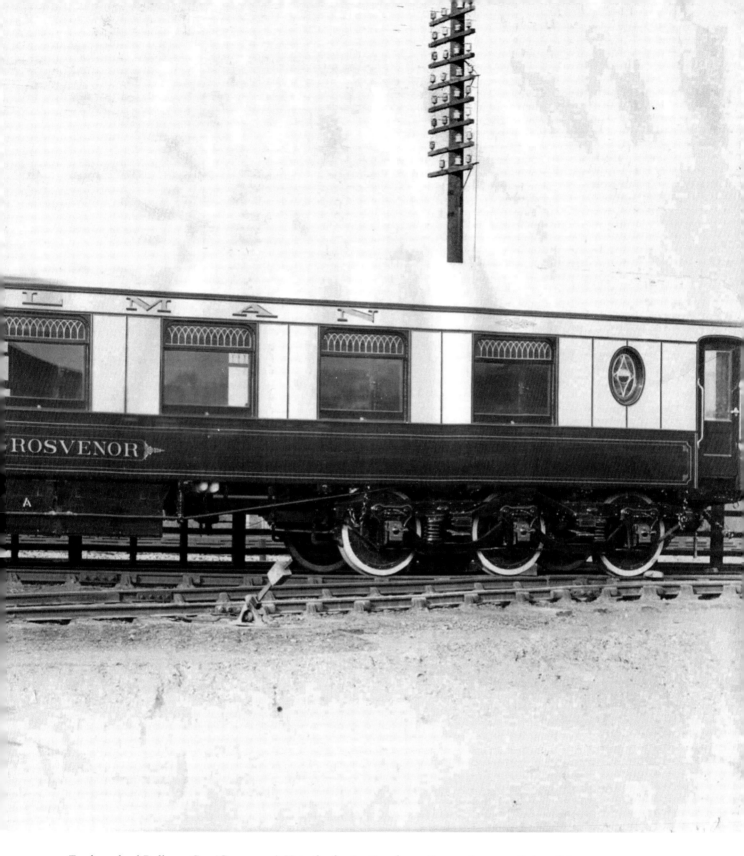

*Twelve-wheel Pullman Car 'Grosvenor'. Note the fascinating decoration on the upper lights of the windows and the 'Georgian' panes on the two windows of the kitchen. Opaque green glass is also prominent in the oval toilet window.*

# BRIGHTON

## PULLMAN DRAWING ROOM CARS.

### ARE RUN IN THE UNDERMENTIONED TRAINS:—

| DOWN. | WEEK DAYS. | | | | | | | | | | | | | | | |
|---|---|---|---|---|---|---|---|---|---|---|---|---|---|---|---|---|
| | a.m. | a.m. | a.m. | p.m. | p.m. | p.m. | p.m. | p.m. | p.m. | p.m. | p.m. | p.m. | p.m. | p.m. | p.m. | p.m. |
| Victoria dep. | 10 5 | 11 0 | 1140 | b | 1 55 | 3/10 | 3 40 | ... | 4 30 | ... | 5 45 | f | 6 35 | 7 15 | 9 50 | 11 d50 |
| London Br. ,, | ... | c | p.m. 1 20 | ... | c | ... | 4 0 | ... | 5 0 | ... | 6 0 | ... | ... | ... | ... | a.m. |
| Brighton arr. | 1124 | 12 0 | 1 0 | 2 30 | 3 0 | 4 10 | 4 45 | 5 12 | 5 45 | 6 5 | 7 5 | 7 15 | 7 40 | 8 45 | 1120 | 1 d8 |

| UP. | WEEK DAYS. | | | | | | | | | | | | | |
|---|---|---|---|---|---|---|---|---|---|---|---|---|---|---|
| | a.m. | a.m. | a.m. | a.m. | a.m. | p.m. | p.m. | p.m. | p.m. | p.m. | p.m. | p.m. | p.m. | p.m. |
| Brighton ... dep. | 845 | 9 20 | 9 45 | 955 | 11 5 | 12/20 | 1 20 | 3 40 | 4 55 | 5 45 | 6 10 | 7 30 | 8 30 | 9 45 |
| London Br. ... arr. | 955 | 1031 | ... | 116 | p.m. | c | ... | ... | ... | c | ... | ... | b | ... |
| Victoria ... ,, | 100 | ... | 1055 | ... | 1230 | 1 20 | 2 20 | 5 3 | 6 17 | 6 45 | 7 32 | 8 57 | 9 53 | 10 50 |

On BANK HOLIDAYS some of the Trains shown in these Time Tables will not be run.
For Particulars see Special Bills.

## Breakfasts, Luncheons, Teas & Suppers supplied in all Cars.

| DOWN. | SUNDAYS. | | | | | UP. | SUNDAYS. | | | |
|---|---|---|---|---|---|---|---|---|---|---|
| | a.m. | a.m. | p.m. | p.m. | p.m. | | p.m. | p.m. | p.m. | p.m. |
| Victoria ... ... dep. | 11 0 | 11 5 | 1215 | 6 30 | 8 0 | Brighton... ... dep. | 5 0 | 5 5 | 9 30 | 9 35 |
| London Br. ... ,, | c | p.m. | ... | c | ... | London Br. ... arr. | c | ... | c | ... |
| Brighton ... arr. | 12 0 | 1220 | 1 36 | 7 30 | 9 35 | Victoria ... ,, | 6 0 | 6 15 | 1030 | 1054 |

b—Saturdays only.　　c—The "Southern Belle."　　d—Wednesdays, Thursdays and Saturdays only.
f—Not on Saturdays

*This page: An interior view of Pullman Car 'Grosvenor', built in 1908. The bar area is just visible through the doorway from the adjoining saloon. Two of the characteristic ormolu and chased metal Pullman table lamps with their pleated silk shades are well seen in this official photograph. Noteworthy also are the elegant, if somewhat impractically small, hat racks and the 'torpedo' lights. Marquetry panelling is made from 'Empire Woods' predominantly used in veneers.*

*Right: Two Cars awaiting formation into a train on a viaduct behind 'Gladstone', number 214. The Car to the right is a 12-wheeler first class Brake Car from 'The Southern Belle'', either 'Verona' or 'Alberta'. It is noticeably higher and longer than the one on the left. This is a third class Brake Car, either Car 25 or 26, which has been converted from a former ambulance coach constructed during the First World War.*

*Above: A characteristically messy consist of a LBSCR train, formed of American built Pullmans (the leading Car is third class No 4), together with a variety of ordinary stock. Leading is 'Baltic' tank No 332, one of seven of similar type and completed at Brighton in March 1922. All seven engines were later rebuilt with tenders.*

*"The Southern Belle" was the first all-Pullman Train in Great Britain. It was inaugurated on 1 November 1908 and was replaced by the electric multiple units of the soon to be renamed "Brighton Belle" on 1 January 1933. The 12-wheel Cars forming the train are shown here on the Crumbles Branch and are being hauled by LBSCR tank engine No 19. The Cars were all English-built in Lancaster; until that time, Pullmans had been manufactured in the United States and assembled in England.*

*A souvenir photograph produced by 'The Pullman Car Company' and 'The Southern Railway of England' in 1929 to commemorate the 21st Anniversary, on 21 November, of 'The Southern Belle". The train is seen behind 'King Arthur' class 4-6-0 No 799 'Sir Ironside'.*

*This page - top: Interior view of Pullman Car 'Alberta' ('Verona').
Note the finely patterned moquette and carving of the free-standing
chairs in the first class saloon, the fleur-de-lys design of the fitted
carpet and some of the rich marquetry panelling.*

*This page - left: Part of the fine decoration on the walls of one of
the Pullman Cars bearing a name with a royal connection -
'Alberta' - which was built in 1908. Note also the torpedo light and
the decoration on the end of a hat rack.*

*Opposite page - top: Interior view of Pullman Car 'Cleopatra'. The
hassocks were unique to Pullman Cars.*

*Opposite page - lower: Interior view of the newly-completed Car
'Bessborough' (there are no signs of scratching or wear). The
window blinds were of damask silk as were the antimacassars. Note
the French ormulu table lamps, the fine decoration in skilfully-
matched grained pear-wood of the walls and partition and the
chased torpedo lights and the hat racks, subtly different from those
in 'Cleopatra'. Schemes of fixtures and fittings were generally
distinct although some were similar in style.*

They are going to Brighton for pleasure. But others are most gay. But young or old, tired or full of health and vigour, all are at their ease, and delighted with this train which provides every conceivable luxury and is exquisite in its artistic decoration.

As the train speeds on its way there is the music of light laughter in the carriages, coffee cups are tinkling, and the sun is gleaming in liquor glasses. Every now and again when the train rushes through a short tunnel, the carriages are made brilliant, and even more beautiful by the little electric lights which glow from the ceilings and the standard lamps on the table – soft suffused light which enriches the colour harmonies of these parlour carriages. Men are smoking cigarettes or cigars, but the cars are perfectly ventilated and the air is always fresh. This fresh air, too, is warmed, and on the coldest day there is no danger to delicate lungs and throats.

So the sixty minutes go by swiftly, and after an experience which is wholly delightful, before any one has begun to feel bored or restless, Brighton is reached, and the travellers find themselves in the city by the sea, with its health giving breezes, its brightness, its gaieties, and its thousand and one attractions.

The "Southern Belle," truly "The most luxurious train in the world," leaves Brighton on its homeward journey, and those who have taken a one-day ticket may return after five hours on the sea front, in the same comfort and elegance and at the same speed.

All these advantages of a swift and delightful journey may be obtained for 12s., the cost of a return ticket.

(The Official Southern Belle publicity brochure 1910.)

*Twelve-wheel Pullman Kitchen Car 'Vivienne', completed in July 1911 and in immaculate ex-works condition. This Car was built by Cravens Ltd of Sheffield for the 'Southern Belle'. It was reported by long standing conductor, Walter Badger, for rough riding and for continual maintenance problems. ('Vivienne' was withdrawn in 1935 following a Board decision to withdraw the heavier twelve-wheelers that had a low seating capacity.)*

*Eight-wheel Pullman Kitchen Car 'Cosmo Bonsor' of May 1912. The Car was built by Cravens Ltd of Sheffield and was painted in 'Red Indian Brown' ('Lake'), instead of the usual Umber and Cream, and had gold lining. The name of the Car was changed later to 'Rainbow'. It is similar to the currently preserved 'Topaz' of 1914. Mr H Cosmo Bonsor was Chairman of The South Eastern and Chatham Railway from 1898 to 1923. He later became Sir Henry Cosmo Bonsor. The photograph shows the vehicle at the SECR Ashford Works.*

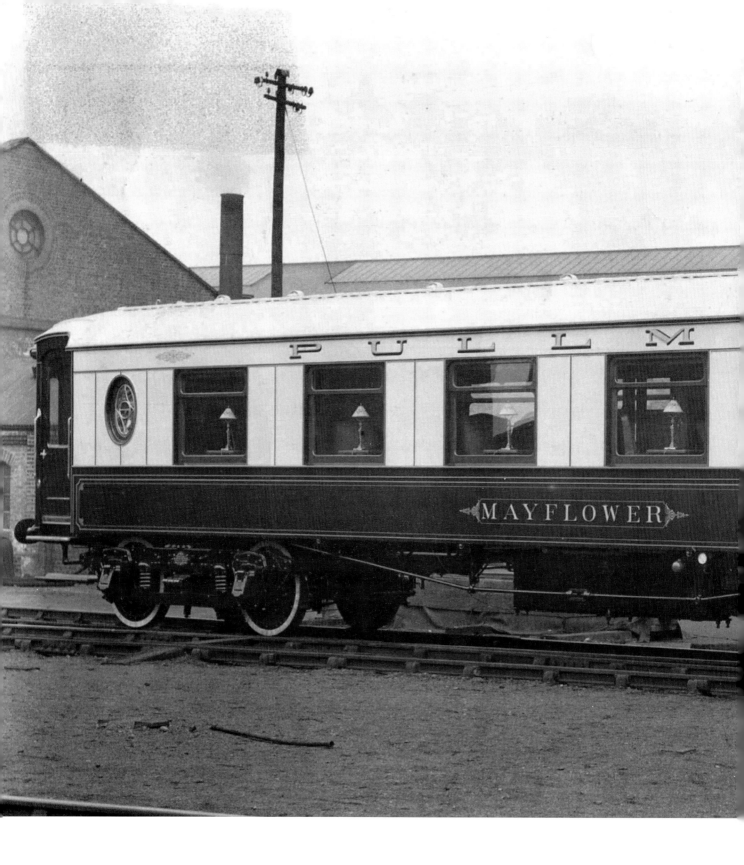

*Pullman Car 'Mayflower', built by the Birmingham Railway Carriage and Wagon Company, went into service on 10 June 1910. She operated with Car 'Galatea' over the Metropolitan Railway and partly over the 'Inner Circle' line between Aldgate and Baker Street and Aylesbury, Rickmansworth and Chesham. 'Mayflower' and 'Galatea' were the names of yachts belonging to Pullman Chairman Lord Dalziel. Both Cars were fitted with a kitchen and a very small bar. Note that there were no gangway connections on the trains. Although there were three oval windows, there was only one toilet, which was locked in the tunnel sections of the Railway. The cars were re-painted later in deep crimson.*

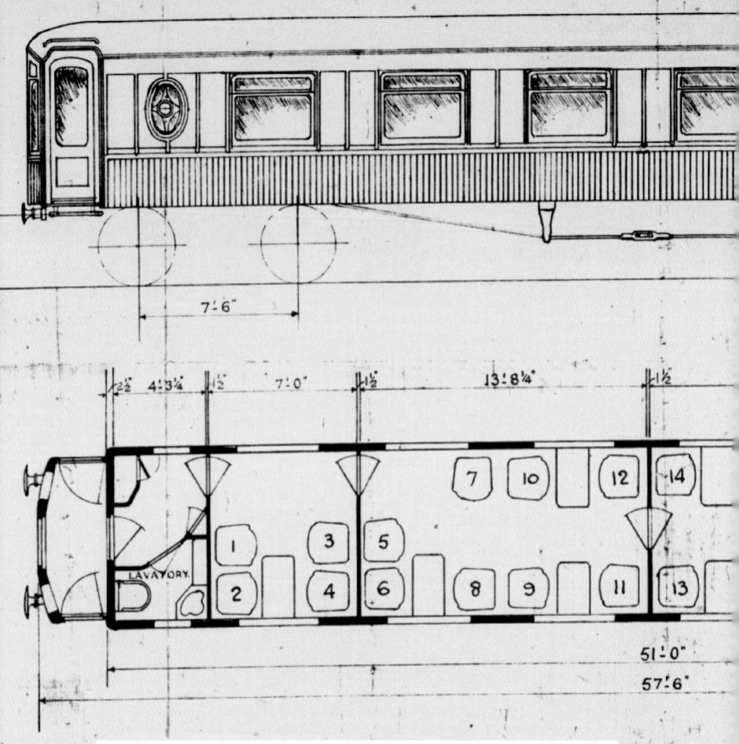

7'-6"

2½ 4'-3¾" 1½ 7'-0" 1½ 13'-8¼" 1½

7   10   12   14

1   3   5

LAVATORY.

2   4   6   8   9   11   13

51'-0"

57'-6"

*Blueprint of the exterior side and end elevations and of the interior layout of Pullman Cars 'Galatea' and 'Mayflower'. The cars began running on the Metropolitan Railway in June 1909.*

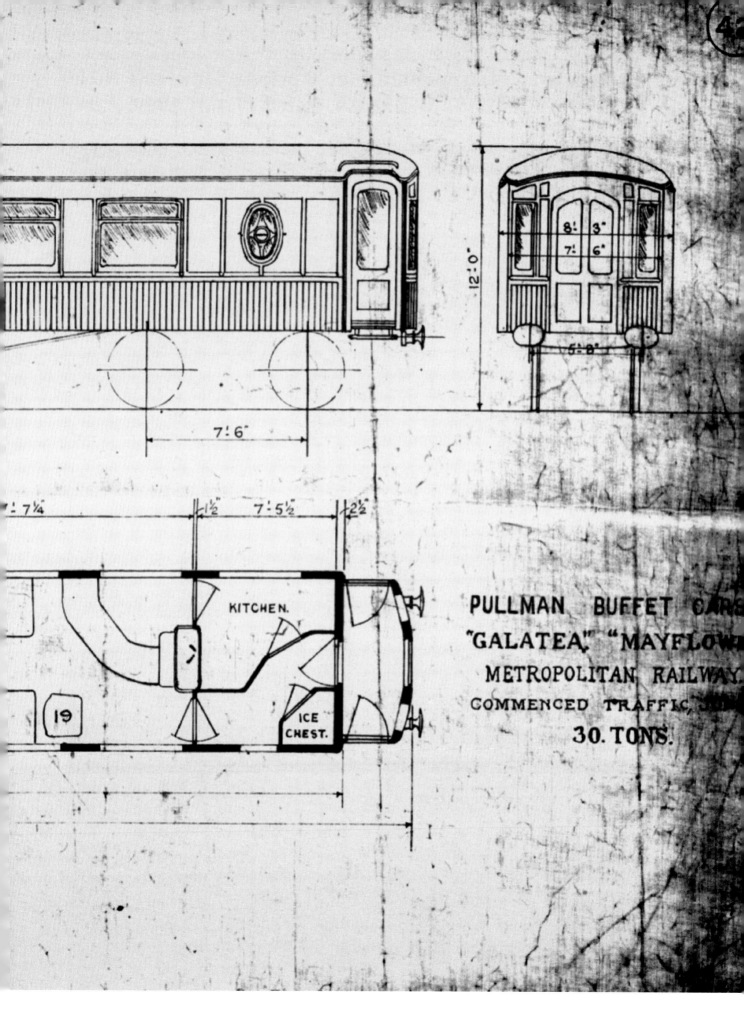

12'0"

5'0"

8' 3"
7' 6"

7'6"

'. 7¼"  1½"  7'5½"  2½"

KITCHEN.

19

ICE CHEST.

PULLMAN BUFFET CARS
"GALATEA." "MAYFLOW
METROPOLITAN RAILWAY
COMMENCED TRAFFIC,
30. TONS.

# Extract from Metropolitan Line Working Timetable No 69
## No 2 Section - Weekdays. Dated 17 July 1939.

**No 1 Service - Saturdays excepted. This Car to work on 9.10 am (No 2 Service) next weekday**

| | | | |
|---|---|---|---|
| M.O. Neasden | Empty | dep | 5.32 am |
| M.O. Baker Street | Empty | arr | 5.44 am |
| M.O. Baker Street | Empty | dep | 5.55 am |
| M.O. Aylesbury | Empty | arr | 7.21 am |
| Aylesbury | | dep | 8.24 am |
| Liverpool Street | | arr | 9.52½ am |
| Liverpool Street | Empty | dep | 10.13½ am |
| Neasden | Empty | arr | 10.37 am |
| Neasden | Empty | dep | 4. 6 pm |
| Aldgate | Empty | arr | 4.36½ pm |
| Aldgate | | dep | 4.44 pm |
| Amersham | | arr | 5.47 pm |
| Amersham | Empty | dep | 6.17 pm |
| Wembley Park | Empty | arr | 6.59 pm |
| Neasden | Empty | arr | 9.40 pm |
| Baker Street | Empty | arr | 9.52 pm |
| Baker Street | | dep | 10.02 pm |
| Amersham | | arr | 10.53 pm |
| Amersham | | dep | 11.02 pm |
| Baker Street | | arr | 11.53 pm |
| Baker Street | | dep | 00.00 am |
| Aylesbury | | arr | 1.22 am |
| | | | Stop |

**No 2 Service - Saturdays excepted. This car and the two carriages detached with it at 7. 5 pm to be attached to train due 7.21 am next day**

| | | | |
|---|---|---|---|
| Aylesbury | | dep | 9.10 am |
| Liverpool Street | | arr | 10.39½ am |
| Liverpool Street | Empty | dep | 10.46 am |
| Neasden | Empty | arr | 11.14 am |
| Neasden | Empty | dep | 4.59 pm |
| Aldgate | Empty | arr | 5.28½ pm |
| Aldgate | | dep | 5.32½ pm |
| Aylesbury | | arr | 7. 5 pm |
| | | | Stop |

# Working of Pullman Cars 'Mayflower' and 'Galatea'.

**No 1 Service - Saturdays only. To Neasden on 7.30 am Sunday morning for attaching to 5.32 am (No 1 Service) on Monday Morning.)**

| Aylesbury | | dep | 8.24 am |
|---|---|---|---|
| Liverpool Street | | arr | 9.52½ am |
| Liverpool Street | Empty | dep | 10.13½ am |
| Neasden | Empty | arr | 10.37 am |
| Neasden | Empty | dep | 12.54 pm |
| Aldgate | Empty | arr | 1.22½ pm |
| Aldgate | | dep | 1.30½ pm |
| Chesham | | arr | 2.50 pm |
| | | | **Stop** |

**No 2 Service - Saturdays only. This Car to work on 9.10 am (No 2 Service) next weekday**

| Aylesbury | | dep | 9.10 am |
|---|---|---|---|
| Liverpool Street | | arr | 10.39½ am |
| Liverpool Street | Empty | dep | 10.47 am |
| Neasden | Empty | arr | 11.14 am |
| Neasden | Empty | dep | 12.24 pm |
| Aldgate | Empty | arr | 12.52½ pm |
| Aldgate | | dep | 1. 0½ pm |
| Aylesbury | | arr | 2. 38 pm |
| Aylesbury | | dep | 8. 17 pm |
| Baker Street | | arr | 9.40 pm |
| Baker Street | | dep | 9.56 pm |
| Amersham | | arr | 10.52 pm |
| Amersham | | dep | 11. 2 pm |
| Baker Street | | arr | 11. 53 pm |
| Baker Street | | dep | 00.00 am |
| Aylesbury | | arr | 1.22 am |
| | | | **Stop** |

'Maid of Morven' was the first Pullman Observation Car in Great Britain. It worked in traffic from July 1914 on the Glasgow to Oban route of the Caledonian railway. The Car was built by Cravens and, as can be seen, had curved plate glass end panels. These were the largest such panels included in any railway carriage and, as such, were easily cracked during shunting. Many spare panels were kept in store in Glasgow ready to replace damaged ones.

*Eight-wheeled Pullman Car 'Princess Margaret'. The clerestory roof and the small, rectangular windows are noteworthy features of this Car. It was also one of the first to have moveable table lamps.*

*A special resolution was passed by The Pullman Company Limited in 1915 to change its name to 'The Drawingroom Cars Company Limited'. Ted had noted at the foot of the document that this was to enable the Company to be renamed 'The Pullman Car Company Limited'.*

## Special Resolution

### THE PULLMAN COMPANY, LIMITED.

Passed ... 15th September, 1915.

Confirmed ... 30th September, 1915.

At an Extraordinary General Meeting of the above-named Company, duly convened and held at 15, Moorgate Street, in the City of London, on the 15th day of September, 1915, the following Resolution was duly passed; and at a further Extraordinary General Meeting, also duly convened and held at the same place on the 30th day of September, 1915, the said Resolution was duly confirmed as a Special Resolution under the Companies (Consolidation) Act, 1908, viz.:—

### SPECIAL RESOLUTION.

"That the name of the Company be altered to 'The Drawingroom Cars Company, Limited.'"

Dated this        day of September, 1915.

Secretary.

*This page: The main saloon of Pullman Car 'Arcadia', built in 1920 by Clayton Wagons Ltd at their Abbey Works in Lincoln. The name of this Car, as that of several others, comes from Greek mythology: in this case, an imaginary place of pastoral happiness.*

*Opposite page - top: Part of the interior of 'Arcadia', built in 1920 showing particularly the handsome cabinet displaying silver-plated cruet sets, sugar bowls and specially wrapped cigars for the Pullman Company. An interesting feature is the brass clock with red and black Arabic numerals. 'Arcadia' was remodelled as Car number 95 in 1934 and withdrawn from service in 1962.*

*Opposite page - lower: Exterior view of the twelve-wheel Pullman Car 'Arcadia' as originally built as a first class Kitchen Car.*

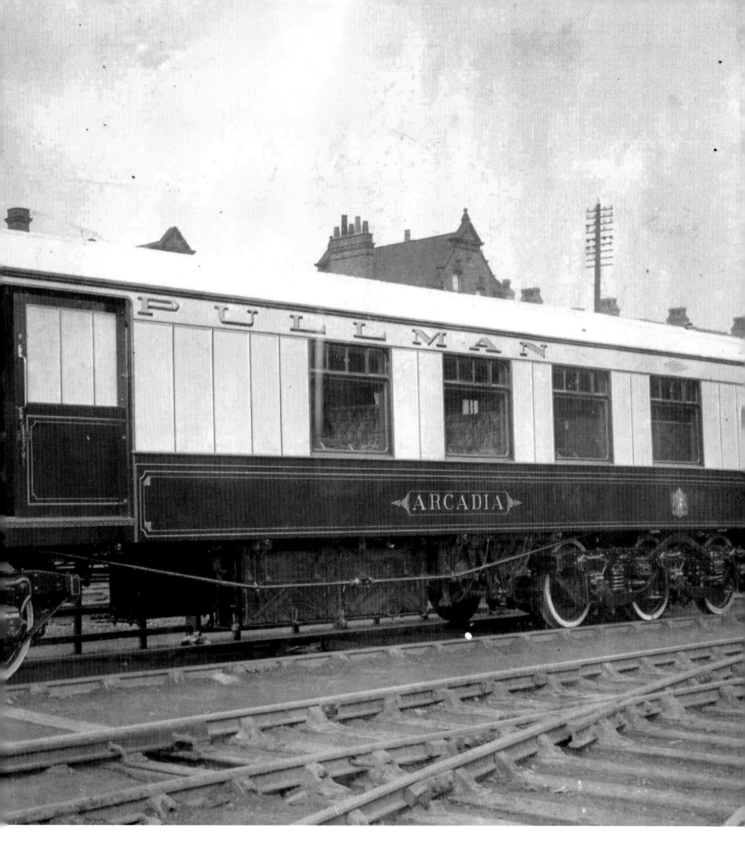

*Twelve-wheeler Pullman Car 'Arcadia' in May 1924, outside the works of the Birmingham Railway Carriage and Wagon Company Limited, Smethwick, where it had just been converted into a Brake Luggage Car.*

*This page: The Coupé in a continental Car, probably serving on the Ostend - Köln Pullman, showing the superb panelling and marquetry work with typical floral motifs. It can be seen that the windows on these Cars were shorter than those in use in England. The table, of a simple design, was very similar in style from one Pullman to another. The continental alarm has instructions in four languages. This Car would have been constructed and assembled in England in 1926 before being shipped to Belgium.*

*Opposite page - top: Another view of the 'Southern Belle' and with Car 25/26 leading. In charge on this occasion is 'B4' class 4-4-0 'Empress'.*

*Opposite page - lower: 'The Harrogate Pullman Limited' train of six Cars and a luggage van hauled by LNER 'Atlantic' locomotive No 1459. The train ran between London Kings Cross and Harrogate. First class Cars would have included 'Rosemary', 'Irene', 'Fortuna' and 'Iolanthe' while the Third Class 12-wheeler Pullmans would have included numbers 46 and 47. However other cars would be substituted if one had been taken out of service.*
*Reproduced from a postcard, which would have been for sale on the train; the photograph was taken by F E Mackay.*

*This page: The apparatus shown is a wireless, apparently an experiment in the 1920s. Just two are known to have been used. Here, Lord Dalziel, Chairman of the Pullman Car Company, who died in 1928, is shown with the bulky receiving and playing equipment. Note the old style table lamp and the overall leather covering of the chairs. The window identifies the Car to be of South Eastern origin.*

*Opposite page: A fine shot of the 'Queen of Scots' all-Pullman train in July 1928 starting away from Kings Cross en route to Edinburgh and being pulled by 'Atlantic' No 4442. The route was extended subsequently to Glasgow Queen Street. The caption on the back of the photograph continues, "The first complete passenger train of 'all-steel' construction to operate in Great Britain". It is likely that this was the inaugural run of the 'Queen of Scots' as everything is clean, the roofs are white and destination boards are included on every visible Car. Note that the Cars are painted cream right up to the cantrail (an umber strip was added in the 1930's above the windows.)*

This page: Pullman Car No 35 of 1926 , part of the 'Golden Arrow' train, receiving some repairs at the Preston Park Works. The carpenter is preparing some mouldings for a table. To obtain the high gloss bodywork on the Cars, 14 coats of paint needed to be applied. When withdrawn from service in 1963, this Car went into preservation at Beaulieu Motor Museum but was subsequently dismantled on site in 1973.

Opposite page - top: Interior view of the first class section of composite Pullman Car 'Grace'. The bulkhead clock and the corridor distinguish the Car from its similar sister 'Doris'. Etchings mounted in black mouldings were by James McBey and Sir D. Y. Cameron. The panelling was in fine English walnut and the decorative effect obtained by the use of convex eagle mirrors cut into fine boxwood. This official works photograph was probably taken in 1932, the year the Car was built. Certainly the carpet and furnishings appear to be in absolutely new condition.

Opposite page - lower:  The All-Pullman Electric Express 'The Brighton Belle' photographed in 1938 on the Quarry Line with set 3052 leading. The Brighton Belle first ran as an electric train in 1933 although its name remained the same as its steam-hauled forerunner, the 'Southern Belle' until 1934. The 51 miles between London and Brighton was covered in an hour. The intensity of the services also changed over the years, initially with three trains in each direction but this was increased later.

*This page: 'The Golden Arrow' pulls away from Victoria Station, London, on its way to Dover in 1946. This was the all-Pullman train's first year of service after its reintroduction following the Second World War. The leading car is 'Lady Dalziel', originally, 'Minerva'. Appropriately unrebuilt Bulleid Merchant Navy Class Pacific 21C1 'Channel Packet' is in charge. The foot of the clock tower of the former Imperial Airways building is partially hidden by clouds of steam from the locomotive.*

*Opposite page - top: W H Smith had a contract with The Pullman Car Company to sell books, magazines and newspapers to passengers at their seats. The hat rack and style of furnishings strongly suggest the photograph was taken in a Queen of Scots car, possibly 'Ursula' or 'Evadne', built in 1928. The table lamp, not original to the Car, is from around 1912, and has a celluloid shade.*

*Opposite page - lower: 'Battle of Britain class No 34086 '219 Squadron' on the 'Golden Arrow', this was Stewarts Lane Depot duty No 3 in 1959. The reason the word 'LEN' is written in chalk on the cylinder is a mystery.*

*Bulleid 'Merchant Navy' Class locomotive 21C1 'Channel Packet' used on the inaugural trip of 'The Golden Arrow' following its resumption between London, Victoria and Dover on 13 April 1946. Note the British and French flags and the large arrow attached to the casing. After the ferry crossing to Calais, passengers transferred to 'La Flèche d'Or', the French counterpart of the service, for their onward journey to Paris, Gare du Nord. Sharp-eyed readers will note these were publicity views of the engine taken at Eastleigh!*

*Cross-Channel Packet, the S S 'Canterbury', owned and operated by the Southern Railway, conveyed 'Golden Arrow' passengers from Dover to Calais on their journeys between London and Paris. The 'Canterbury' is seen here alongside Dover Quay in April, 1946. She began service in 1929 at the same time as the 'Golden Arrow' service was introduced and was later used in the Dunkirk evacuations. She was finally broken up by a Belgian scrap merchant in 1965.*

*This page: Exterior of the Trianon Bar Car which formed part of 'The Golden Arrow' train. The inclusion of the two arrows and the words 'Golden Arrow' and 'Flèche d'Or' on the sides of the 'Arrow' Cars meant that the Pullman crests had to be positioned right beside the Car doors. This Southern Railway photograph was taken in April 1946.*

*Opposite page - top: Pullman Car 'Diamond' built in 1925 and forming part of 'The Golden Arrow', showing the Trianon Bar in the background. The photograph was taken in April, 1946. Compare the 'contemporary' design of the post-war moquette on the chairs with the more traditional designs used earlier in the Century. The Car later served on 'The South Wales Pullman' as the 'Daffodil Bar.'*

*Opposite page - lower: 'The Trianon Bar' Car was available to all passengers on the train irrespective of their class of ticket. The Southern Railway photograph was taken in April 1946, and was apparently posed for this publicity 'shot'.*

This page: The final 'Trianon Bar' shown here was part of first class Car 'Pegasus', built in 1951 specifically for 'The Golden Arrow' and to commemorate the Festival of Britain. The sliding lights of the Car windows are noticeably deeper than on earlier vehicles. The restrained design of the separate marquetry work panel, taken from Car No 5, showing English oak and French vine leaves, contrasts with the more elaborate work seen in earlier Cars. Note the magnificent stylised aluminium map panel behind the Bar showing Eros' golden arrow linking London and Paris. (Interestingly, Stanley Adams was Chairman of an aluminium company as well as Chairman of Pullman.)

Opposite page - top: The bar section of 12-wheel Car No 5 'The Trianon Bar' Car. The clean, gleaming lines created by modern design and the new plastic materials cannot have worked well under even the light usage of this Car. Note the laminated Pullman coat of arms above the display of cigars and cigarettes.

Opposite page - lower: General view of the first 'Trianon Bar' (Car No 5) seen from the lounge section after its extensive makeover in 1946. Laminated plastics, a then innovative material, were used for re-surfacing the walls, bar and table tops in a colour scheme of grey, pink and cream. The curtains were in pink plastic; one wonders how long they remained in this immaculate condition. Stanley Adams was a director of Bakelite Limited, manufacturers of the plastics used in this Car.

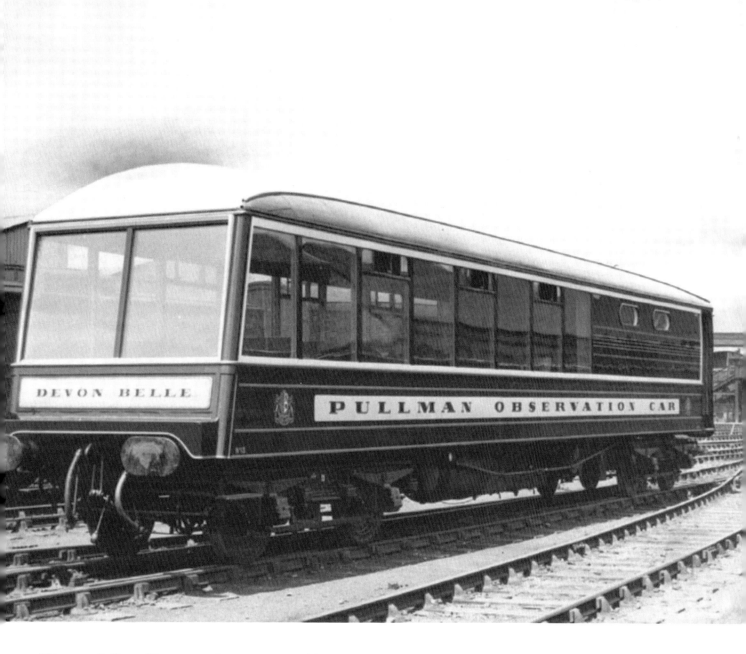

*This page: Pullman Observation Car, reconstructed from a 'J' type Car, either 13 or 14, for use solely on the main portion of the 'Devon Belle'. This all-Pullman train ran from Waterloo to Barnstaple and Ilfracombe and a separate portion initially, to Plymouth. Of course, a visit to the turntable was required for this Car after each journey.*

*Opposite page - top: The 'Devon Belle' nearing the end of its journey on Barnstaple Bridge in July 1947. All Cars, save the Observation one, are of the 'K' type.*

*Opposite page - lower: The all-Pullman 'Devon Belle' service leaving Waterloo on 2 September 1947 behind 'Merchant Navy' 35013 'Blue Funnel'. The 1949 supplementary fare for the service was Waterloo to Exeter 6/- First Class and 3/6d Third Class, Exeter to Plymouth 3/- and 1/6d respectively, and from Waterloo to any other destination served by the train 8/- First Class and 4/6d Third Class.*

*One of the two Observation Cars converted specially for the all-Pullman 'Devon Belle' train from third class 'J' type Cars. Publicly the 'Belle' ran non-stop between Waterloo and Exeter Central, although a stop was made purely to change engines at Wilton, west of Salisbury. At Exeter Central it divided with one portion going to Barnstaple Junction (five hours 33 minutes from Waterloo) and the other to Okehampton and Plymouth Friary (five hours 36 minutes). Variations in train running times occurred over the short period of the life of the Belle. The down service (from Waterloo) ran on Monday, Thursday, Friday, Saturday and Sunday and the up service on Monday, Tuesday, Friday, Saturday and Sunday during the Summer and until late September. The photograph was taken outside the Company's works at Preston Park, Brighton.*

This page: Rebuilt 'Merchant Navy' Class, No 35022 'Holland America Line' leaving Southampton Central with the down 'Bournemouth Belle'. The stock consists of a variety of 12-wheel Pullmans of 1920s vintage together with Car 303 of 1952 just visible by the platform canopy.

Opposite page - top: Rearward looking, interior shot of a 'Devon Belle' Observation car. The magnificent views obtainable from these Cars as they sped through southern counties countryside may be appreciated in this 1947 photograph. Seats were made to swivel and were made harder than those of the Cars in the rest of the train to encourage visitors to the Observation Car to limit the time of their visit! Light fittings were of celluloid with a 'go-faster' stripe.

Opposite page - lower: Interior view taken in 1947, of one of the 'Devon Belle' Observation cars. The photographer was looking towards the vestibule leading back into the train. A large pictorial map of part of the route is on the Car bulkhead, behind the curved settee. Drinks could be purchased from a small bar. Passengers were at liberty to use seats on a 'first come, first served' basis, moving to and from their booked seats elsewhere in the train.

*This page: The Hull portion of the 'Yorkshire Pullman' recorded at Hull Dairycoats and formed of four 'K' class Cars. Taken circa 1955, the engine is 'D49' No 62763 'The Fitzwilliam'.*

*Opposite page - top: The Master Cutler' Pullman express en route from Sheffield approaching Brookmans Park Station on its inaugural run to King's Cross, London on 15 September 1958. The cars forming the train had been transferred from the Southern Region and were all first class save for two second class brake Cars. Later, one or two additional second class Cars were added, subject to demand. The train was the first diesel-hauled Pullman and has Type 4 (later Class 40), 2,000hp diesel-electric locomotive D207 in charge.*

*Opposite page - lower: Chairman of the Pullman Car Company Limited, Frank Harding, chats to two travellers before the inaugural run of 'The Master Cutler' or, as the train was known for the midday run only, 'The Sheffield Pullman'.*

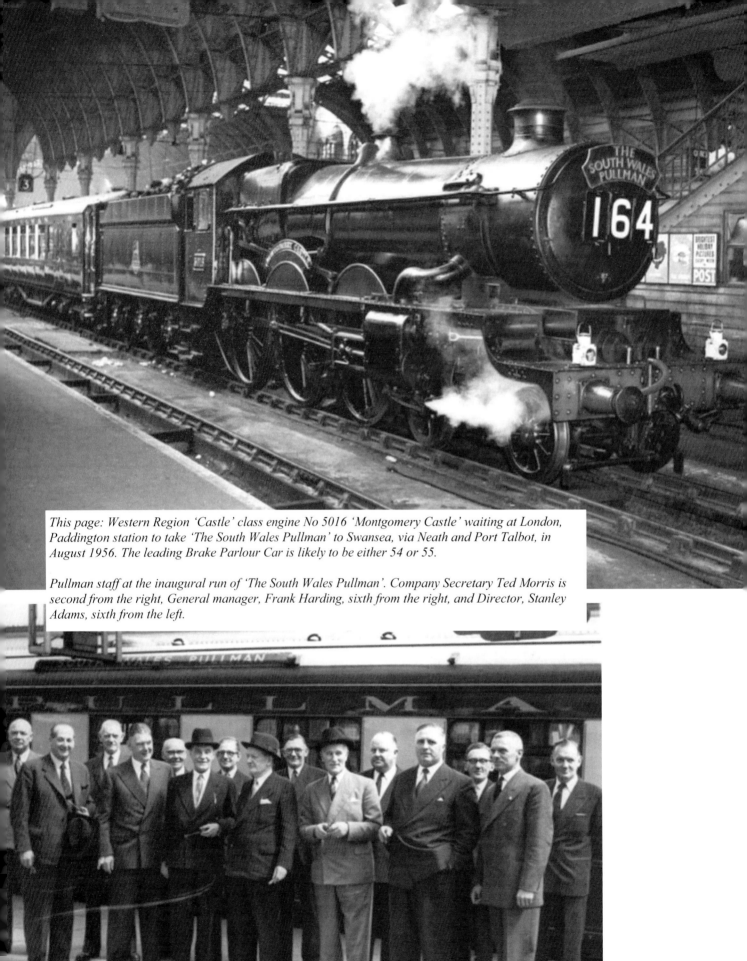

*This page: Western Region 'Castle' class engine No 5016 'Montgomery Castle' waiting at London, Paddington station to take 'The South Wales Pullman' to Swansea, via Neath and Port Talbot, in August 1956. The leading Brake Parlour Car is likely to be either 54 or 55.*

*Pullman staff at the inaugural run of 'The South Wales Pullman'. Company Secretary Ted Morris is second from the right, General manager, Frank Harding, sixth from the right, and Director, Stanley Adams, sixth from the left.*

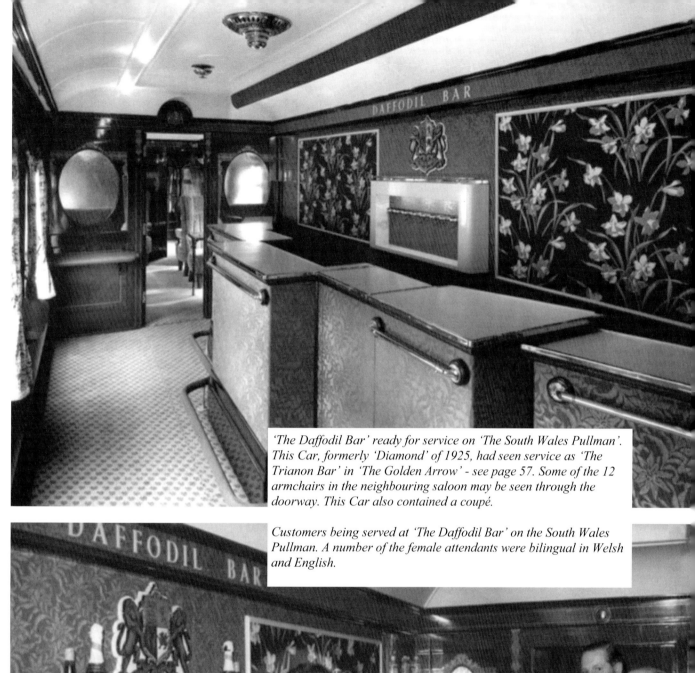

'The Daffodil Bar' ready for service on 'The South Wales Pullman'. This Car, formerly 'Diamond' of 1925, had seen service as 'The Trianon Bar' in 'The Golden Arrow' - see page 57. Some of the 12 armchairs in the neighbouring saloon may be seen through the doorway. This Car also contained a coupé.

Customers being served at 'The Daffodil Bar' on the South Wales Pullman. A number of the female attendants were bilingual in Welsh and English.

'Pullman Car, 'Phoenix', built in 1952, posed outside the Company's Works at Lovers Walk, Preston Park, Brighton. Note the post-war Golden Arrow practice of having a rounded-corner rectangular toilet compartment window instead of the usual oval one. 'Phoenix' used on royal trains was said to be a favourite car of Queen Elizabeth the Queen Mother. The running gear for 'Phoenix' was originally fitted to 'Rainbow', a 'Bournemouth Belle' Car destroyed by fire in 1936.

*This page: Interior view of First Class Pullman Car 'Phoenix'. Note the splendid collage panels designed by Mary Adshead including a group depicting two of the four seasons and a central panel showing a vintage steam locomotive. The moquette was black and white and although the lamps were much simplified they sported plain white shades of an experimental design.*

*Opposite page - top: Second Class saloon of Pullman Kitchen Car 338 built in 1961 by Metropolitan Cammell Carriage and Wagon Company Limited. This type of interior was equivalent to first-class rolling stock of British Railways of the time.*

*Opposite page - lower: Coupé of a First Class Pullman Parlour Car, built by the Metropolitan Cammell Carriage and Wagon Company Limited in 1960 and put into service later that year or in 1961. Note that the lower part of the interior walls are covered with rosewood veneer. All the oxidised metal lamps are fixed and have white opaque glass lampshades and incorporate a criss-cross pattern. Part of the table folds down to allow easier access to the moveable seats which are of different design to those in the saloon. The 'aircraft-style' luggage / umbrella racks are in oxidised metal to match the lamps. (See page 76).*

*First Class Pullman Parlour Car 'Emerald' built in 1960 by Metropolitan Cammell.*
*Also shown is Second Class Pullman Parlour Car No 349, one of seven built in 1961 as part of a 1960 order for 44 similar vehicles, known appropriately as the '1960 Metro Camm Cars'.*

*This page: Interior of First Class Pullman Car 'Emerald' built in 1960 and showing the clean, spartan lines of design typical of the time as the railways attempted to compete with the airlines. It is interesting to compare features with those shown in interior views of Cars built earlier in the Century; here are the redesigned arm-chairs and 'luggage' racks, the swan-necked table and wall lamps, concealed wall and ceiling lights, glass panels, and anodised metal finish and plain wood panelling devoid of any marquetry.*

*Opposite page: The caption on the back of the photograph reads, 'Relaxing in a Pullman Car, awaiting tea service en route to the North of England.' The wide sliding light above the main window identifies this as a 1920s Car. There is also a hint of marquetry behind the model. There are green and red dragons on the curtains and cut moquette upholstery on the winged armchair. The 'Whispering Grass' crockery was introduced in 1961/2.*

*This page:  In 1960 British Railways in conjunction with Pullman introduced a diesel multiple unit Pullman service between London St Pancras and Manchester Central, and also between London Paddington and Bristol / Birmingham. Known as the 'Blue Pullman' trains due to their striking colour scheme, six-car sets were used on the Manchester Central trains, and eight-car formations for the Western Region services. Later (in 1961) an additional service was run between Paddington and Swansea under the name of 'The South Wales Pullman' and replacing the steam service illustrated previously. This is an eight car set forming the South Wales service at speed in Sonning Cutting sometime in the mid-1960s. The Venetian blinds have been let down in some of the windows. Notice also the roller-blind destination board fitted in the side of the power car. The original of this photograph was hung on the wall behind Ted Morris's desk.*

*Opposite page - top: Personal service in the ultra-modern surroundings of a 1960s Blue Pullman. White-gloved attendants serve passengers with lunch as a Midland Pullman train speeds on its way to its destination. Some of the attendants had transferred from British Rail to Pullman services on both the Midland and Western Regions and they became quickly loyal to Pullman ideals. The winder for the venetian blind, which operated between the two panes of glass, may be seen on the extreme right. There are two buttons either side of the table lamp - one is the light switch, the other for calling the attendant. The chairs were adjustable; the white knob on the lever is just visible by the attendant's left knee. Tablecloths were of 'Terylene' and 'Pullman' on the napkin is in red thread.*

*Opposite page - lower:  Westbound Bristol Pullman diesel multiple unit passing St Anne's Park Station, Bristol in 1960. (George Heiron / Transport Treasury)*

# BIRMINGHAM PULLMAN

Last Journey

Paddington to Birmingham

3rd March 1967

## Wine List

| | Bottles | ½ Bott. | ¼ Bott. |
|---|---|---|---|
| | 40/- | 20/- | 10/- |
| N.V. | 19/- | 10/- | 6/- |
| | 40/- | 13/- | 6/- |
| | 26/- | 10/- | 6/- |
| | 19/- | 10/- | 6/- |
| | 26/- | 13/- | 6/- |
| | 19/- | 10/- | 6/- |

### SHERRY

| | |
|---|---|
| Tio Pepe | 4/- |
| Bristol Cream | 4/- |
| Amontillado No. 4 | 3/9 |
| Walnut Brown | 3/9 |

### LIQUEURS IN MINIATURES

| | |
|---|---|
| Fine Old 4/- | 6/3 |
| Crème de Menthe | 6/3 |
| Heering's Cherry Brandy | 6/3 |
| Wolfschmidt Kümmel | 6/3 |
| Benedictine | 6/3 |
| Drambuie | |
| Cointreau | |
| Gin Proprietary Brands | |

Gold in two-fifths Gill Measures

Sold in one-fifth Gill Measures

| | 2/5 |
| Worthington "Green Shield" | |
| Guinness    Mackeson | |
| Tuborg Lager | |

| | 2/10 |
| | 1/6 |
| Whiteway's | |

### MINERALS

| | |
|---|---|
| | 1/6 |
| | 2/6 |
| | 10d |
| | 10d |
| Pepsi-Cola | 1/6 |
| Vichy Celestins | |
| Lime Juice Cordial | |
| Orange Squashes | |
| Fruit Juices (assorted) | |

### CIGARETTES

Player's Medium    Player's Gold Leaf Filter

Wills Embassy    Rothman's King Size Filter    Piccadilly Filter

Sterling    Benson & Hedges King Size

Leading Havana Cigars    Manikin Cigars    Wills Castella Panatellas

Churchmans' Grandee Short Panatellas

## Afternoon Tea

### 4/6

...d Teacake

...Assorted Sandwiches

...White Bread & Butter

...rves    Swiss Roll    Biscuits

...t of Tea

## High Tea

### 10/6

...nd Bacon

or

...t and Salads

or

...pped or French Fried Potatoes

...Rolls and Butter

...iscuits    Swiss Roll

...ot of Tea

*Please ask for a bill and retain it*

In case of difficulty with passengers please see the Conductor or write to the
General Manager, British Rail Catering, 14 Bishop's Bridge Road, London

*Opposite page - top: 'Bristol Pullman' 1964, composed of 'K' type Cars from 1923 vintage behind a 'Western' class diesel. These vehicles were seldom used in the mid-1960s, and were deputising for a 'Blue Pullman' unit requiring maintenance.*

*Opposite page - lower: Birmingham Pullman menu card - the original was printed in Royal Blue on white, for the last journey of the Western Region Blue Pullman service between Paddington and Birmingham Snow Hill on 3rd March 1967. After this date services between the two centres would be concentrated on the line from Euston and the former WR route relegated very much to that of a secondary line. Oh, for an afternoon tea for 4/6d, or a lager for 2/5d!*

*This page - right: Cartoonists Lee's commentary in 1954 on a possible outcome of British Railways finally absorbing Pullman Cars into its operations. This was the occasion of the Company shares being taken over by the British Transport Commission. A rather overweight, shabbily turned-out attendant, chained teaspoon in hand, roars down the gangway, "Now then Sir, hurry up! Another gent here wanting the spoon."*
*Reproduced by permission of The Associated Newspapers Ltd, London.*

*This page - lower: One of the last memorandums, the original typed then stencilled and duplicated, sent by Ted Morris before his retirement and circulated to all Pullman Car, Supplement and Deluxe Services staff in January 1967 a few months before his retirement. His devotion to service to the Company, which was fostered among and shared by all employees, is clearly evident in the note.*

### BRITISH RAIL CATERING PULLMAN DIVISION

To: All Pullman Car and SDL Services Staff                                        Paddington Station January 1967.

As you are all aware there is a changing pattern of operation of Rail services, a greater development of the Inter-City services, and in this connection it has been decided by the Board to regionalise control of Pullman Car trains, and the important Restaurant Car services.   This means that the Pullman Division, as such, will cease to exist.

I am retiring from the Service, but I am confident that you will give the same loyalty to the particular officer under whose control your train or refreshment vehicle may now become.

The new arrangements are planned to become fully effective well before the start of the new Time-Tables to be introduced on 5th March next.

I propose to retain my interest in you all by being one of your passengers on as many occasions as I am able.  I know from experience that you will not fail to give me the full satisfaction of good service as you have given and will continue to give to our passengers.   The million passengers travelling Pullman in a year, and the many times that number who receive service of refreshments in other catering cars are proof indeed, if it is needed, that our services are much appreciated by the travelling public.

There is nothing to beat the satisfaction of giving good service.  I am proud to have been connected with this aspect of British Rail travel for so long.

E J Morris Manager

This page: The former Pullman Car 'Queen Margaret', Number 219, built in 1927 and allocated to the former Caledonian Railway area. It was sold in 1933 to the LMS and became a restaurant car. 21 other Cars were sold to the LMS at the same time. 219, 220 'Kate Dalrymple' and 221 ' Helen of Mar' were retained in service on the Scottish Region where this photograph was taken in September 1964. The vehicle would appear to be being re-supplied with water.

Opposite page - top:Pullman Cars surplus to requirements were sometimes retired as 'Pullman Camping Coaches'. A new conversion from a 'J' class Car, possibly the former 'Coral', poses in the chalk cutting outside the Preston Park Works. Many of the 'J' class Cars had been used as hospital carriages in the First World War and afterwards purchased by the Company and converted into Pullman Cars. When the Cars became redundant and withdrawn from service, many were burned although some, including 'Elmira', 'Maid of Kent', and 'Formosa', survive in preservation.

Opposite page - lower: Pullman Camping Coach interior showing the simple accommodation available in one of the twin-bedded cabins. The iron bedsteads were manufactured specially for the Coaches while the carpet is the original one. The oval window shows that this cabin was at the vestibule end of the Car where there would have been a toilet and corridor. Part of the original marquetry work and decoration may just be seen on some of the woodwork. This is possibly Car 'Coral'. Customers were able to pay for the hire of their Coach when they bought their rail tickets.

# THE VIP's CHOICE

*Opposite page - top: A Royal Pullman occasion at London Victoria station in the late 1940s, with King George V1, Queen Elizabeth, Princess Elizabeth and Princess Margaret. The Car is probably 'Rosemary'*

*Opposite page - lower: His Majesty King George V1 being welcomed at Victoria from the royal train on 12 May 1947. The Queen is just stepping down from their Pullman. The Prime Minister, Clement Attlee, waits, top-hat in hand, to greet the King*

*This page: King George V1 and other members of the Royal Family including Princess Alice, welcome a visiting monarch ( - King Frederick 1X and Queen Ingrid of Denmark) to Britain from his Pullman train at London Victoria station, Tuesday 8th May 1951.*

*The Queen arrives at Tattenham Corner by Pullman train with the Queen Mother, Princess Margaret and the Duke of Edinburgh for a day at the races. The distinctive shape of the kitchen window identifies the Car behind the royal party as 'Aries' of 1952.*

*Above: The departure of Her Majesty The Queen Mother by Pullman train from Waterloo Station on 20 October 1954 en route for the United States of America and Canada through the port of Southampton. The Queen and the Duke of Edinburgh and their children, Prince Charles and Princess Anne together with Princess Margaret are there to bid her 'Bon voyage'. The Prime Minister, Winston Churchill, is also visible. Pullman attendant Hawkes stands smartly behind the Duke of Edinburgh. The Queen Mother is about to board a Car borrowed from the 'Golden Arrow' train.*

*This page: Prime Minister during the Second World War, Winston Churchill, in characteristic pose in the coupé of Pullman Car 'Joan' in 1941. 'Joan' was at the disposal of Churchill on nearly all occasions for his journeys around Britain. At other times, other cars deputised, most notably, 'Philomel'.*

*Opposite page - top: Prime Minister Churchill and his wife, Clementine, alighting from their Pullman Car.*

*Opposite page - lower: Former President of the United States, Dwight D Eisenhower, waves to onlookers from his seat in 'Joan' in 1962. Note the rather extravagant late 1950s style of curtain material.*

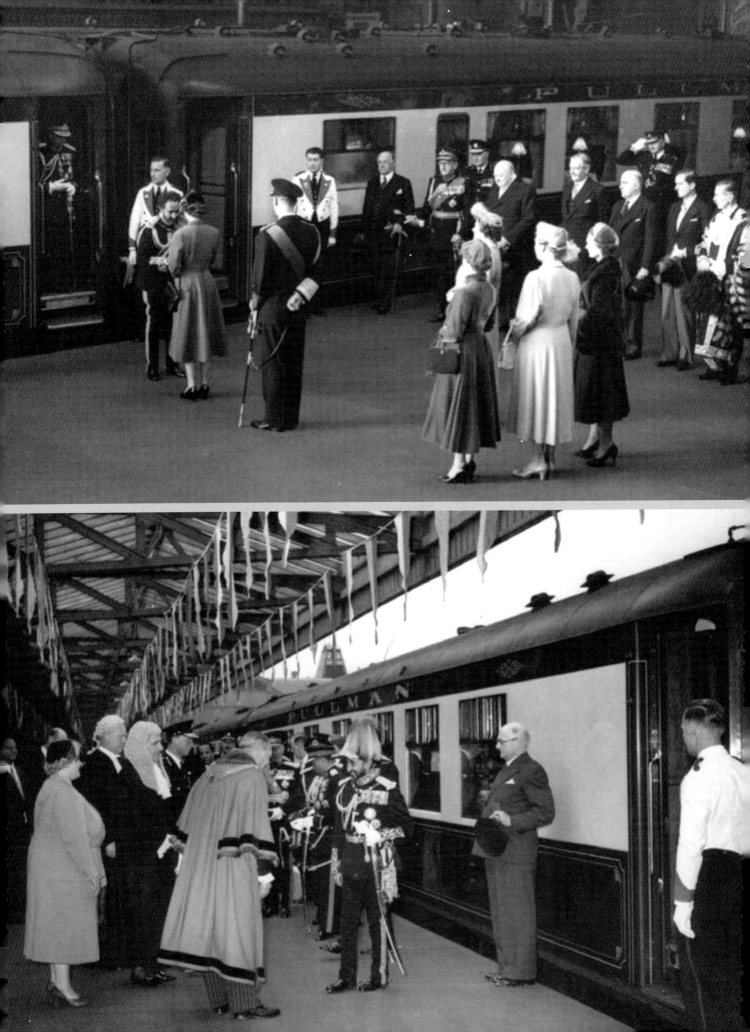

*This page: Smartly turned out Pullman Car attendants in the 1950s await the arrival of visitors to their train which, according to the roof board on Car 'Gwen' is to be used for an 'International Reception' (- held at the Metropole Hotel, Brighton). The Cars seen here at London Victoria formed part of 'The Brighton Belle'.*

*Opposite page top: Emperor Haile Selassie of Ethiopia received a royal welcome at London Victoria in October 1954. Included in the line-up of VIPs are the Prime Minister, Winston Churchill, and Foreign Secretary, Anthony Eden.*

*Opposite page - lower: Emperor Haile Selassie, having arrived in his Pullman train is greeted by a civic dignitary on 14th October 1954 during his state visit. The Car dates from 1951 and saw service with the 'Golden Arrow'.*

*Above: J Arthur Rank starlets, Peggy Evans and Patricia Daynton, stand on the step of one of the Pullman Cars forming the 'Queen of Scots' in 1948. The train was about to leave from Leeds on the remainder of its journey to London. This was the first post-war run after eight years of enforced 'retirement'. The two starlets and another starlet, Rona Anderson - later to marry Gordon Jackson - were passengers on the train's run from Glasgow to London. Gordon Jackson had in fact flagged away the opposite working from London, Kings Cross the same day.*

*Opposite page: A typical state visit to Britain of the Fifties, on this occasion the Monarch was King Feisal of Iraq, with dignitaries being welcomed by the Queen, the Duke of Edinburgh, Queen Elizabeth the Queen Mother, the Duke of Gloucester, Princess Alice and other members of the Royal family from their Pullman train at London Victoria. The date is 16 July 1956. The Prime Minister, Anthony Eden, other MPs and Government officials also form part of the welcoming party. Car 'Orion' and would have brought the visitor from Dover Marine. This occasion was also just 10 days before the start of the Suez crisis.*

*This page: The smart Pullman leading \attendant, hair well brylcreemed, waits to take a traveller's order. Lapels and cuffs were vibrant blue while the gold braid 'epaulettes' denote the senior ranking of this attendant. Bow ties were normally favoured items of uniform rather than an ordinary tie. The rectangular badge on his right lapel displayed a unique number intended for the use of passengers when communicating with the Company. Unique numbers were also engraved on the reverse of the Pullman Crest badges. The heavy velour above the attendant's head and behind his left side was used in the gangway connections between cars as a draught excluder.*

*Opposite page - top: State visit of the Shahanshar of Iran on 5 May 1959. He is being welcomed from his Pullman train at London Victoria by The Queen, Duke of Edinburgh, and other members of the Royal Family, politicians and other dignitaries.*

*Opposite page - lower: Former French President, Charles de Gaulle, has just arrived by Pullman train at the Night Ferry Platform at London Victoria for a state visit in April 1960. The car nearest the camera is Golden Arrow Car 'Phoenix'. Special stands were erected on the platform for the press and those specially invited at such occasions.*

*With best wishes*
*Tony Hancock*

*The late Tony Hancock, radio and television comedian, has the Pullman Car attendant in stitches over the brandy. Did Pullman cars ever run near Railway Cuttings, East Cheam? (Photograph presented to Ted Morris in the 1960s.)*

*Left: Ted Morris, extreme right, with well turned-out Pullman staff whilst on the 'Kosygin Special' close to the time of his retirement in 1967. The interior shows this to have been taken in a 'Golden Arrow' car. At the front to the left is the senior attendant Reg Varney who was always seconded to Royal Special trains.*

*Right: A smartly turned-out 'Golden Arrow' car attendant probably from the late 1940s or early 1950s. Only 'Arrow' Cars were identified by numbers and had the Pullman crest close to the door of the lower panel. On the reverse is the legend, 'His Majesty The King said in his Coronation Broadcast on May 12 1937, "The highest of distinctions is service to others." Ted helped the Company maintain the highest of standards during his years with Pullman.*

This page: Contemporary LBSCR advertising of 'The Southern Belle' depicting Car 'Belgravia'.

Opposite page: Pullman Cars from the diverted 'Bournemouth Belle' at Fareham on 1 November 1964. Nearest the camera is second class Pullman Car No 76 of 1928. (John Bailey)

Lower views - both pages: Taken from the LBSCR advertising booklet on its Pullman services dating from circa 1908. The heavily retouched and colour tinted views give a good impression of the early Pullman vehicles running on the line. They are - opposite page top - left to right, 'Princess Patricia', 'Duchess of Norfolk', and 'Princess Ena'. The original view was recorded on the Crumbles siding.

THE MAXIMUM OF LUXU[RY]

(DUCHESS-NORFOLK)

## "PULLMAN" and "PERFECTION"

Are synonyms when they refer to Car Building, in which art the Pullman Company leads the world.   In elaborate design, substantial construction and luxurious finish, Pullman Cars represent the highest standard of excellence.

Ingenuity and skill are constantly being applied to the improvement of details with a view to adding to the comfort of travel.   Every Car is in charge of an experienced, well-trained Conductor, whose services are always at hand from start to finish of a journey, and invalids and ladies with children can always rely upon ready attention to their comfort and convenience.

Cleanliness is also a special feature, coupled with perfect ventilation and good lighting, thus making travelling a real luxury.

## THE *MINIMUM* OF COST.

## PARLOUR AND BUFFET CARS RUNNING BETWEEN LONDON AND BRIGHTON

### Length, 63 ft. 8½ ins.     Seating Capacity, 32.

These Cars are available to holders of First Class Tickets by payment at the Booking Office, or to the conductor in charge, of ONE SHILLING for each seat occupied, or SIXPENCE for any distance not exceeding 26 miles.

Seats can be reserved to order upon application to the Superintendent of the Line, L. B. & S. C. Railway, London Bridge Station ; the Station Superintendents ; or the Manager of the Pullman Company, Ltd., London Bridge Station.

✿   ✿   ✿   ✿

Arrangements can be made for the reservation of Pullman Cars for Private Parties at special rates.

# PULLMAN

*Marie Dornier, Miss France 1966, poses with railway officials alongside a Blue Pullman First Class Car. The various expressions amongst the staff are priceless.*

# PRIDE